Ana Blair

The Art Of Being A Woman

By: Ana Blair, M.Ed.

Ana Blair

Copyright © 2018 by **Ana Blair**

All Bible texts in this publication are quoted from the King James Version (KJV) unless otherwise noted. All rights reserved. This book or any portion thereof may not be reproduced or used in any manner whatsoever without the express written permission of the publisher except for the use of brief quotations in a book review.

ISBN E-13:978-0-9974857-8-3
ISBN-13: 978-0-9974857-4-5

Pataskity Publishing Company

Augusta, Georgia

Introduction

Being a lady has many challenges. We often struggle internally during our childhood, and such struggles may enter into adulthood. For each woman, our problems may be different or similar; however, what is a common factor regardless of our barriers or issues is that God cares for us. God's love is promised to us, and he can full any empty void within our lives. The purpose of this book is to discuss the various issues and changes that women experience, and how to succeed in overcoming such challenges from a Christian perspective.

In this book, I have reflected on many of my personal experiences to educate women of all backgrounds how to develop a relationship with the monotheistic God. God wants to be closest to us. Our circumstances are not our own. Let's read about the many women who were in unwanted situations, but still found moments to trust in God. You may not see yourself in each woman, but you may see yourself in at least one of these biblical characters. I pray while reading that you are embraced with wisdom, and learn how to overcome. During moments when you feel most broken, trust God.

Thanks for reading!

This book is dedicated to women of all ages, especially young girls who will grow up and become women. I dedicate this book to you!

With all sincerity,

Ana Blair

Ana Blair

Guide To Reading

Introduction	7
Loving Yourself and Your God	2
My Child, I Hear	14
I Long To Be Like You:	16
A Story Of Ruth & Naomi	16
Aptitudes of Faith	19
Pray this prayer with me my friend:	23
Seasons Change	26
Making the Best of a Bad Situation:	27
A Look Inside the Life of Abigail	27
A Rose	34
Beauty Is Skin Deep:	35
A Discussion of Queen Esther	35
They're Talking	41
I Was Raped and I Am Broken	42
Treasures In You	48
Treasures In You-continued	49
Protecting What Is Yours Story of Miriam and Moses	50
Strengthen The Good That Remain	54
When God Speaks To A Woman A Discussion of Deborah	55
I Dwell In You	57
Be Hospitable: A Shunammite Woman Blesses Elisha	58
Sister, Live and Live Again	61

Sister, Live and Live Again- continued 62

Conclusion 63

See Yourself As God Sees You

Scourged with pain and unacceptance,

So deeply scarred that even once grown it was hard to find deliverance.

It hurts being tainted by others' thoughts and concepts

It becomes easy to feel regret.

I have to remember that we are shaped in iniquity,

But God gives us a unique identity.

"I will praise thee; for I am fearfully and wonderfully made: marvelous are thy works; and that my soul knoweth right well."

Psalm 139:14

Loving Yourself and Your God

Love is a word that it is often misunderstood and misquoted. Due to the usage of the word, its meaning has become vague and difficult to ascertain. One may ask, "What exactly is love?" It is a four-letter word that took me several experiences to define. When I think of love, I do not immediately assimilate the thought with those who are hurting and are in need. People of certain socio-economic status, and the fact that they may lack being loved are not my initial thoughts. Regardless of how rich or poor one may be, we all need love. While we may only consider the fact that we may need love, the need is universal. Everybody needs love especially those who are hurting.

Jesus taught us to show love to those who are in need. I ask myself, "Has my view or understanding of love been tainted somewhat by society's depiction of love?" Many people in today's society have the wrong imagery or idea about love. Our understanding of love may have been affected by what is observed in society each day. Essentially, society has changed not only how we see love, but how we give and receive it. We must be careful concerning love, and be vigilant how we seek it and give it.

The reason being is because the meaning of love has been plagued with incorrect ideas and concepts. With so many definitions of the word love, I would like to refer to the Bible to seek a meaningful definition. I ask myself, "How does the Bible define love? What does God have to say about the definition of love as it is defined in its original Biblical context?" Although love is one word, there are three types of love. The three types of love are agape, eros and philos. Even if one refers to the Hebrew translation of love, the original language of the Bible, the translated word is "Ahava." The meaning of Ahava is, "I give," and, "love;" therefore, love is an action word. Let's look at a more explanatory definition of love. The following addresses the three types of love.

Agape is the type of love that God the Father has for humanity. It is the type of love that Jesus the Son of the Living God has for humanity, as well. This is not the type of love that we can earn, or that can be bought. This is a self-less love that is ongoing, and is a gift to us. Despite one's wrongdoings, this type of love will persevere because it is an ongoing love.

Eros is a type of love that refers to one person being intimate with someone else, or having a physical attraction that one would have for a spouse or companion. Eros is a romantic type of love.

Philos is a type of love that we have for our friends and is used when developing friendships.

"Love suffers long and is kind;

> love does not envy;
> love does not parade itself, is not puffed up;
> does not behave rudely,
> does not seek its own, is not provoked..."
>
> **1 Corinthians 13:4-5**

So often women may attempt to wholeheartedly love someone while love has not been properly defined within their lives. Being women, we not only long to love someone; We often long to love someone else while failing to love ourselves. If love means, "I give," and we love ourselves first during our childhood and adolescent years, we should have given ourselves love before we give our heart, material things, and even our body to someone else. For example, how can one promise to be patient and kind to a lover while one has not been patient in kind with their self. Regardless if it is healing from past experiences, working to complete college, or even creating stability in the work world, my sister, love yourself enough to treat you kindly and patiently first; build the best version of you that can exist. Yes, love is important, and you will fail at loving anyone until you have truly loved yourself.

Because we have discussed love means, "I give," love is never defined by selfishness or greed. Love is not defined by haughtiness, fashion, cars or one's material possessions. These things have absolutely nothing to do with love. In fact, these behaviors are the opposite of love. It is an undesirable relationship if two people are together only for materialistic gain.

Love is like a bare essential. It is without form. One of the earliest exemplifications of love in the Bible is demonstrated between two naked people named Adam and Eve (Genesis). The fact that they were without clothes or material possessions alone demonstrates that love needs nothing to exist because it is a natural feeling. Adam and Eve did not learn of themselves being naked until each were corrupted with sin: "And the eyes of them both were opened, and they knew that they were naked; and they sewed fig leaves together, and made themselves aprons" (Genesis 3:7). It was not until then that both immediately became ashamed, and hid from each other. The scripture states that they even hid from God: "And they heard the voice of the Lord God walking in the garden in the cool of the day: and Adam and his wife hid themselves from the presence of the Lord God amongst the trees of the garden" Genesis 3:8. My friend, it leaves me in awe how we can become so comfortable with ourselves, our mate, and even our lives until sin eats at our lives. When we are living in holiness and sanctification, there is never a reason that we ought to be ashamed. In a pure and honest relationship, there is never a reason that we will be ashamed. But in that moment when ungodliness creeps in, we ourselves may behave just Adam and Eve and hide from the ones whom we love.

We should love with a pure heart, and have an attitude of openness and honesty in all our relationships regardless if it is a personal or interpersonal relationship. Jesus taught in the scripture to love thy neighbor as thyself: "And the second is like, namely this, thou shalt love thy neighbor as thyself. There is none other commandment greater than these" (Mark 12:31). This is interesting because it establishes an idea for self-love. For example, apply the following text from 1st Corinthians 13 to how you feel about yourself.

Love is patient....

Be patient with yourself. Your dreams may not become true, or a reality as quick or soon as you would like it too, but be patient with you. Love in the meaning of *Eros* may not exist yet in your life, and this may cause you to feel frustrated, but be patient with yourself. If you are still searching for the right companionship, be patient with yourself. Whenever you treat yourself with patience, and become appreciative of where you are at this moment in life these are characteristics of loving yourself.

Love is kind....

A smile is so much more beautiful than a frown. On your good days, on your not-so-good days, be kind to you. Perhaps treat yourself to something sweet to eat, and walk downtown alone. Enjoy a warm bath and movie time. Those are just some ideas of how you can be kind to yourself. It is essential to your overall well- being that you appreciate who you are, and do kind gestures for yourself.

Love does not envy....

Between you and I, every woman can become a little jealous at times; however, we should never be envious of each other. We do not have to be envious of one' achievements. If you properly endure each stage of life, you will never envy the manifestation of God's work in someone else's life. The reason being is because you will know first-hand, or through your personal experiences that the struggles are very challenging in life; thus, for anyone to overcome them is a miracle. Whenever we do not envy other people, it is an indication that we are content and grateful for our lives; therefore, we are loving ourselves when we behave in such manner. The world is already dark and gloomy on certain days, so let us be the light that inspires, uplifts and encourages our sisters.

Love does not boast, is not proud, it does not dishonor people…

Love is not proud. Various reasons may cause us to believe that love consists of pride. This is not correct. We are not supposed to brag about ourselves while in relationships. We should not be too proud thinking too highly of ourselves because we have attained a certain career, education, or even overall success. We are to be modest, and pass along any type of hope and knowledge to the next woman. As we love ourselves, we freely give love to others.

Love is not self-seeking…

As women, we all have a self-seeking nature. It is normal to say: "mines, mines, mines, or me, me, me!" So frequently, we may develop a selfish attitude throughout life. Regardless if we created such selfishness because we felt overlooked, manipulated, cheated, abused or neglected, it is not a good to be overly concerned with ourselves and less concerned about others. There are several causes why one may create a self-seeking nature. When we are self-seeking, we only seek self-glory. Instead we should be seeking God's glory.

"But lay up for yourselves treasures in heaven, where neither moth nor rust doth corrupt, and where thieves do not break through nor steal:"

Matthew 6:20

"And the world passeth away, and the lust thereof: but he that doeth the will of God abideth forever."

1 John 2:17

Love is not easily angered; It keeps no records of wrongs....

Do you know anyone who is mal tempered? Are you short tempered? Does it seem that people anger you to the point that he or she does not deserve forgiveness? If so, I have been there. But it is not godly to become easily angered, and to keep this anger for days then the days become weeks, next the weeks become months, suddenly the months become years. You are such a beautiful woman. How can you ever see the fullness of your beauty if your coloring it with ongoing anger?

"To appoint unto them that mourn in Zion, to give unto them beauty for ashes, the oil of joy for mourning, the garment of praise for the spirit of heaviness; that they might be called trees of righteousness, the planting of the Lord, that he might be glorified."

Isaiah 61:3

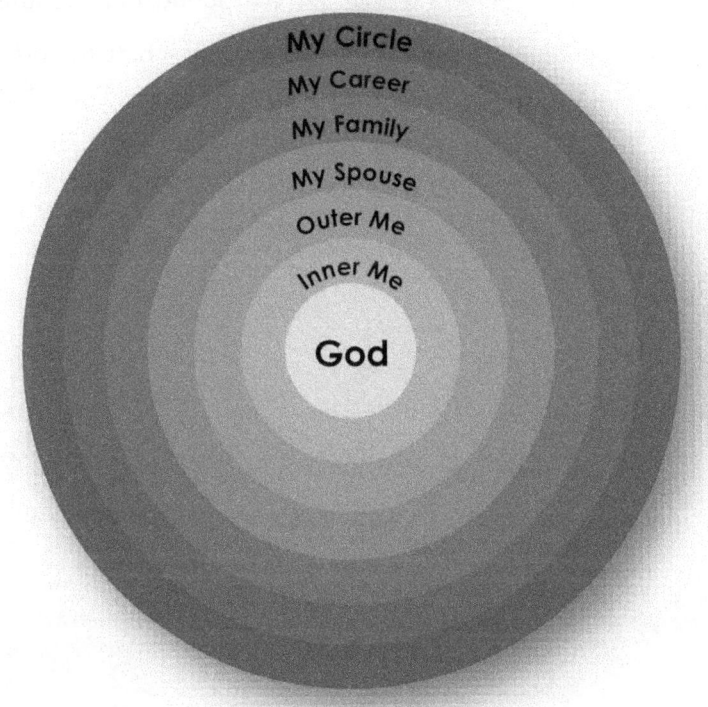

Provided is a chart that demonstrates how I prioritize matters and feelings of the heart. This chart provides in detail how love initially starts with God. If you noticed God is the center of this chart; he is the core. I remember growing up and being asked: "How can we love a God whom we have never seen, but cannot love the people here on Earth and we see them daily?" This question often resonated with me, and reminded me we cannot love ourselves, or love anyone else until we have made a connection with the creator and love him.

If we love our creator, we will love all people and love ourselves. Love yourself while protecting your heart, hopes, and dreams. Always believe in the plans that God has for you. Do not fail to love yourself. Once you fully and completely love yourself, you will be able to live an abundant and fulfilling life. You will be able to love all people. You may use the chart to sort of such feelings, priorities and so forth.

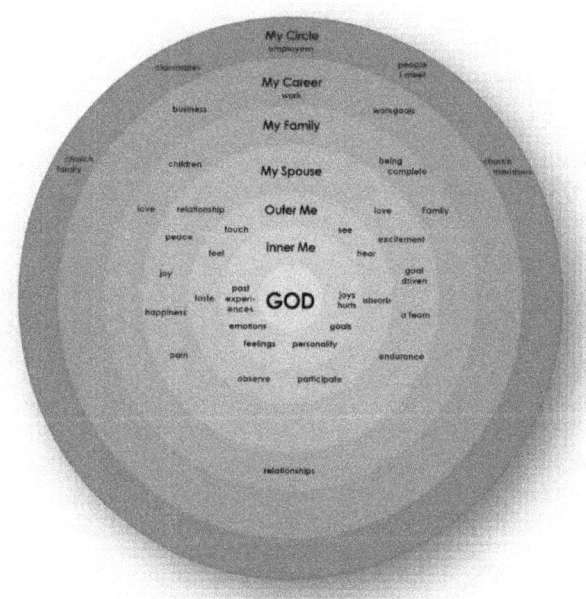

The diagram below demonstrates matters. This diagram will help you put matters of the heart, emotions and people whom are in your life into perspective. Whenever organizing what I refer to as the strings of the heart, keep in mind that you are connected to God. He reveals to you his plans for your life, and he will take away any negative issues from your past if you just give him the control to do so. He not only cleanses you, and forgives you of your yesterdays, but also he gives you hope for your future.

During my college years, I searched to define myself as many women do during those earlier years of life. We search for who we are, and who we can potentially become in our future. Being a full- time college student while working, time management became very important to me. Very soon, I learned that there are certain things I have time for, and some task I had to put off until a later time. Time management is very important.

Let's discuss the chart. We will start from the center where there is God. With so much prioritization, I placed orders in my life, and I knew that God had to be first. Jesus states in Revelation 1:8: "I am Alpha and Omega, the beginning and the ending, saith the Lord, which is, and which was, and which is to come, the Almighty;" therefore, I knew if I was going to be successful in my endeavors, I needed to place Christ as my first and greatest concern.

Understanding this diagram or graph is essential to me to organize my feelings. Because we are women, we understand that we can become more open when reacting to emotions or from an emotional place. It is best to have a guide or an idea for how we feel, what we feel, and what order those feelings should be placed. We not only have the option to organize our feeling, but also we can organize our goals, task, obligations, people and so forth. I encourage you if necessary to make a diagram, as well, and organize your own emotions just as I have. In your chart or diagram, you can demonstrate how God is essential and how his love works inside of you; thus, appealing through you. Change begins from within. If you have a spouse, you may place your spouse on the chart as well. Then, decide where is your family will be placed alongside deciding placement for work, career, and goals. Afterwards, determine where anyone else in your life will be located on chart. This type of activity has helped me, and I am sure it will help you. It is beneficial to have the matters of our heart, feelings, and emotions placed into perspective.

Now that the first matter of business is taken care of, let us move forward to explore several dynamic women in the Bible whose lives and stories can and will inspire us!

The art of being a woman is knowing God and who you are in him; it is to live and exercise wisdom that you may become as God sees you.

My Child, I Hear

Every time I close my eyes

A new wave catches me by surprise

The world we are living in

Why couldn't it just be dead to sin?

Why do I have to fight so hard?

Just to be ripped apart...

I need an epoch

A resurrection; a new start

God, are you there?

My praying is sincere.

I need to know you care.

You promised my burdens you will bare

God, are you there?

My Child, I Hear-continued

And Jesus says:

"Yes, my child I'm here

Yes, my child I hear

Like I promised, I will always be here

To show how much I care

But you must learn how to trust

Even when things aren't looking up; even when things aren't looking up"

I Long To Be Like You: A Story Of Ruth & Naomi

Aconcern I have is when women sometimes use scriptures, tradition, or certain values to indicate why they do not have to labor. For various reasons, I have never believed that a woman does not have to work, or do any type of labor to contribute to her family's well-being. The Bible teaches us about the dangers of being lazy in Proverbs 6:6: "Go to the ant, O sluggard, observe her ways and be wise;" thus, the scripture uses an example of how the ant works and prepares for her well-being. This scripture alone speaks to those who are sluggard and lazy, teaching them to work. The scriptures also imply while there is plenty of work to be done, there are few workers.

One of my former teachers once told me: "A man washes his face, but a woman washes her house." This saying remained with me as I realized how important a woman's role is to her family, and how much her strength is depended upon. I would never suggest that a woman should over rule a man. We understand she is the weaker vessel, exemplified here: "Likewise, ye husbands, dwell with them per knowledge, giving honor unto the wife, as unto the weaker vessel, and as being heirs together of the grace of life; that your prayers be not hindered (1st Peter 3:7). Because of this scripture, we know a woman is not to be overpowering to the man; instead, she is to be a helpmeet. However, that does not mean that as women, we should not contribute anything to the well-being of ourselves and our family. We should be our children's and husband's cheerleaders; we should encourage and pray for our families. We must take on the role of service, love and patience within our families.

It is unfortunate that many homes are broken, or will fail because of the foolishness of a woman. It is our responsibility to use wisdom to make solid and logical decisions not only for us, but also for our household. Have you ever heard of a free ride? Why is it that so many of us want to have a free pass through life? Why is it so many times a female may want a to ride on a man's successful coattails when she is indeed capable of taking care of herself? My beloved, this type of behavior should never be acceptable. Do not attempt to get everything for nothing. Do not be a woman who goes through life looking for handouts without any desire to work. This is not ladylike, and it is not being a woman of good character. For a woman to go through life without any sense of knowing herself, or aptitude to get up and create something out of her life is deprivation not only to her, but also to those who surround her.

Finances are a huge cause for divorce rates. Because divorce rates are already skyrocketing, you do not want having insufficient finances to become a cause of your divorce. You may ask, "What can prevent this from happening?" My response will be, "Work! Work! Work!" There is a saying that I always use, and it is very popular it says, "Work Hard, Play Hard!" Always be willing to work and provide for yourself.

While a lot of men expect a woman to work, there are some men who do not have this expectation. Certainly, live by the standards of your husband, and be submissive to him. If your husband prefers that you work as a homemaker, that is understandable. By being a homemaker, or a stay at home mother you are working. Trust me, I know from experience that motherhood and being a homemaker is laborious and you should be proud of your labor. However, for those of us who are not wives, who work as mothers, do not have an agreement with our spouse to not work, or are single, we should be working. Have enough appreciation for life to take care of yourself. God will reward you for doing so.

Aptitudes of Faith

Sometimes we work from pain

Sometimes we work for all we may gain

We are like a clover just waiting to unfold

To reciprocate the glories life beholds

What pushes us to move forward

May in each reason be different

But the ability to dream then work for it

Is a priceless ambition

All are aptitudes of faith

To work and multiply is truly divination

"But my God shall supply all your need according to his riches in glory by Christ Jesus"

Philippians 4:19

I want a Boaz! I want a Boaz! I have heard women on numerous occasions talking about how much she wants a Boaz which means a husband who can and will provide. The scripture teaches us to love each other as we love ourselves. Taking a look inside the life of Ruth, we understand she was not someone who desired to avoid work and live a life of laziness. The significance of Ruth's life story is that she not only followed her heart, but also whenever opposition occurred in her life, she responded to her hardships with the dedication to work.

Ruth was born a Moabite which means she was born a Gentile. As we may know through previous studies, people who were Gentiles were regarded as sinners, unsaved, or even unclean. However, Ruth did not allow the fact that she was a Gentile to determine her destiny, nor destroy the outcome of how she lived her life. In Ruth's heart, she wanted more spiritually than what she knew. She desired to know and love the monotheistic God. Because Ruth longed to be redeemed, she became very affectionate towards her mother-in-law, Naomi. Naomi was an Israelite, and she was a servant of God. Because of Naomi's ongoing and unwavering relationship with God, Ruth decided that she will always follow Naomi.

Once we are saved, we are always saved despite the hardships that we may experience. Ruth's pursuit to love God caused her to inherit a new life. Ruth's life is a representation of the sinner, or the unsaved individual who finds Christ. Naomi and her husband, Emilech lived in the Land of Moab because famine drove them out of the land of Judah. After ten years, Naomi was not only saddened because of the death of her husband, but also bereaved because both of her sons had passed away. Neither of Naomi's sons had children; therefore, Naomi did not encourage their wives to remain with her. Instead,

Naomi encouraged her two daughters-in-law to return to their home. Oprah, Naomi's daughter-in-law, returned to her homeland.; however, Ruth did not return to her homeland.

Per Ruth 1:16, when Naomi expressed her concern that Ruth should leave her, Ruth responded, "Intreat me not to leave thee, or to return from following after thee: for whither thou goest, I will go; and where thou lodgest, I will lodge: thy people shall be my people, and thy God my God;" thus, indicating Ruth's willingness and desire to follow Naomi. Ruth traveled with Naomi to the land of Judah, as stated by Ruth to Naomi. In a society like Moab that was full of pagan worship, it is interesting to know Ruth's willingness to leave her homeland and travel to the foreign land of Judah with her mother-in-law.

Although Ruth no longer had a living husband, and she never bore any children it is amazing what our love for God will compel us to do. Once Ruth and Naomi arrived in the city of Judah, Ruth had to go to work. She picked wheat and barley so that she and Naomi had food to eat. However, this scenario was dangerous for Ruth as she was a foreigner and a widow; she could have been raped while working. Ruth had no covering, protection, or a man to look after her in the unknown land of Judah. Foreigners and people of lower socio-economic status could pick wheat or barley from the end of the field, and that is where Naomi instructed Ruth to work. Despite all the excuses Ruth could have made, she made a sacrifice to place her fears aside and work to care for her and Naomi. Ruth's actions exemplify courage and wisdom.

Interestingly, in life it behooves us to deal with obstacles just like Ruth. When we overcome various feelings such as fear, hurt, pain, disappointment, and even sorrows by getting up every day to put one foot forward, we are creating our pathway for success. I admire Ruth's courage to follow the God that she so deeply believed in, but also to stick closely by him whenever challenges occurred. Beloved, learn from Ruth. Stick to what you believe even when troubles come in your life.

As women, we are created in beauty and strength; however, when obstacles occur and things are as bad as we think things can be, do not ever give up. Keep going; keep trying, praying believing, and when you are tired of doing all the above work, watch, and wait. Sometimes even the strong can become weak. The Bible teaches us to be weary not in well-doing, and to not faint when it says, "And let us not be weary in well doing: for in due season we shall reap, if we faint not" (Galatians 6:9). In other words, do not quit. You are only human, and it is understandable that there will be times when you feel tired, but do not quit. Wait and while you are waiting on God to change your circumstance, do not let go of your hopes and your dreams. Do not let go of the hopes and dreams that God placed in your heart.

Moving forward is very important. Ruth gave her best even when life brought her the worst. Have you ever noticed anyone who can be up when things are up, but they are down when things are down? We should never behave in response to a situation, or circumstance. Be stable, conducive and productive in bad times as well as good times. Be prayerful in all situations.

Pray this prayer with me my friend:

Majesty, Eternal and Universal Father,

Today, I pray to understand pain.

Sometimes tragedies are placed in my life for me to grow stronger.

Lord, teach me how to not respond to the brokenness of life with bitterness and frustration. Instead, make me susceptible to your will and your plans as you mentioned in Jeremiah 29:11.

Whatever is good for me and my walk with you, I pray to enter it.

Whoever is not good for me and my walk with you, I pray to release them from my heart.

Bless me with grace that even when I do not know your will.

I pray that I still walk in your will

Because my life is yours!

I pray you have the glory in Heaven.

Amen

While Ruth was working in the field, Boaz inquired about her. He was curious about Ruth because she was beautiful, but a foreigner who risked her life to work to provide for her mother in law and herself. How impressive! It was even more appealing that Ruth stuck so closely by Naomi even though Ruth's husband died. Such behaviors demonstrated Ruth's commitment and loyalty even in a tumultuous situation. Boaz saw a woman who did not fail to live beyond standards, remaining dedicated to her situation. Boaz saw strength in Ruth. Only because of these behaviors, Boaz felt compelled to offer Ruth wheat and barley each day. The characteristics that people see in us each day should be strength and patience. Do not go wrong because life is not going right. Someone may be watching you. It may not be Boaz, but someone may be observing your actions and your response to life's situations.

Ruth gained love and security because of Boaz. She had enough to eat and shared plenty with Naomi. Boaz assumed responsibility of Ruth by promising that she will always have food to eat, and he also told the other field hands which he owned to look out for Ruth. Ruth was invited to eat lunch with the workers who were from Judah, and she felt accepted.

In conclusion, Boaz marries Ruth, and they bore a son named Obed. Naomi loves and nurses this son, and Naomi loves Ruth and Boaz. Ruth was as much help to Naomi as any son would have been in those days. Eventually, Ruth would become great-grandmother to King David. This story teaches us that we can begin with a small action of faith, but create miracles and exceed our own expectations even as our faith is tested.

NOAMI

God became the center of her life

She loved her husband, sons and daughters in law

God restored her joy that was lost due to her deceased family.

RUTH

Loved God and desired to be saved

God converted her life because of her faith and desire

Blessed her destiny

Seasons Change

What does it mean when seasons change,

And things become rearranged?

What does it mean when you see the fall falling into winter,

And the winter winds into spring

Then into summer, but fall comes soon again

When life's sun not only arises, but it also sets

When we find that we have failures, but made success

When people come in, and out of our lives

Some to no one's surprise

What does it mean when life never stand still

But it goes on

Clothes, furniture and things become rearranged

And the seasons change?

Making the Best of a Bad Situation:

A Look Inside the Life of Abigail

Through the life of Abigail, we experience learning about a woman who made the best out of a bad situation. Abigail was a beautiful woman. Per 1st Samuel 25:3, she was beautiful inside and out as it is written, "Now the name of the man was Nabal; and the name of his wife Abigail: and she was a woman of good understanding, and of a beautiful countenance" Abigail possessed wisdom and courage alongside being physically attractive. During the period of history in which Abigail lived, marriages were arranged. Thus, Abigail did not choose her husband, Nabal. The union to him was arranged without the consent of either party.

During Abigail's marriage, she experienced very challenging times because Nabal was verbally abusive and foolish. Abigail found herself in a bad situation. The name Nabal means, "to behave foolishly, or to be a fool." Nabal was a very wealthy man who had a bad temper, and was known to disrespect others. If I had not known that Abigail's marriage was arranged, I would have wondered the cause for such a beautiful woman to live in in what was obviously a miserable marriage. Because marriages were pre-arranged, it can be presumed that for some reason, Abigail's parents approved of her marriage to Nabal. Perhaps, her parents believed it would be best for her to be married to Nabal because of his wealth, and the financial security that he could have offered Abigail. The reason Abigail was married to him is unknown, but what we do know is that she was married to Nabal, and she was in an unhappy situation. Despite being unhappy, she attempted to make the most of a bad situation.

Unlike Abigail, we have the freedom to choose our spouse. We choose our husbands because we could accept or decline their proposal for marriage. Most women live their lives waiting to be asked the magical question: "Will you marry me?" Frequently as women we find ourselves caught up in relationships that are not healthy to our well-being in an effort to get married. Sometimes we even recognize these issues prior to marriage, but because of the overwhelming desire to be married we tend to overlook the same issues while we are dating. The scripture informs us that Abigail never blamed herself for being in her predicament, but she prayed for Nabal.

She committed to loving her husband despite his arrogant, evil, and, selfish ways. Abigail made a conscious decision to be faithful before God. In our lives, we make choices daily. Like Abigail, we should be willing to be faithful to God in good and bad situations. Some circumstances we created, and other situations life created. Being consistent and faithful are some of our greatest qualities. For example, we accepted our spouse's flaws prior to marriage, but during the marriage we agonize dealing with each other's flaws. Because we made a vow before God, we have to be faithful to that commitment. Ecclesiastes 5:4 states further, "When thou vowest a vow unto

God, defer not to pay it; for he hath no pleasure in fools: pay that which thou hast vowed;" thus, if you made God a promise, please keep it.

While the scripture teaches us the importance of keeping a commitment, we should deal knowledgably with each situation, and not partake in abusive relationships, confusing them for a healthy relationship. We should not live in harm's way or be physically and mentally violated in any of our relationships. A healthy marriage is essential to the procurement of a Christian family. Always pray for your spouse. Pray for their faith to remain strong, and that they do not fail God, as the Bible dictates, "But I have prayed for thee, that thy faith fail not: and when thou art converted, strengthen thy brethren." (Luke 22:32) As believers in the body of Christ, we pray for the strength and faith of other believers. We should be praying this same prayer for our spouses because sometimes each of us will become weak in our faith.

I am certain that Abigail became weak at times and was unhappy due to the selfishness of Nabal, but she approached her situation with positivity. Abigail prayed for Nabal; she begged for his life to be spared when Nabal rebelled against King David. These actions alone demonstrated Abigail's commitment to her marriage, strength, courage, and wisdom. Abigail did not respond to her already negative situation with evil actions. She instead behaved righteously.

David whom had already been appointed by King Solomon to lead Israel commanded Nabal to provide lambs for a feast. In 1st Samuel 25:10, Nabal denies David's request, stating, "And Nabal answered David's servants, and said, Who is David? and who is the son of Jesse? there be many servants now a days that break away every man from his master." Nabal not only denied

David, but also made a joke of David's request to receive lambs. David felt Nabal should have provided lambs for the following reasons: David's power grew, and he had already been appointed to be King; David protected Nabal's lambs and land. It was tradition for wealthy men to pay the King, or provide what the King requested. Nabal had a foolish attitude, and responded to the men of David's army foolishly.

When David's men brought him the words of Nabal, David was furious. How dare Nabal insult the King! 1st Samuel 25:13 states, "And David said unto his men, Gird ye on every man his sword. And they girded on every man his sword; and David also girded on his sword: and there went up after David about four hundred men; and two hundred abode by the stuff." David was on his way to kill Nabal because of Nabal's foolishness. Abigail heard of this, and immediately, without her husband's consent or permission, prepared gifts for David as written here, "Then Abigail made haste and took two hundred loaves of bread, two skins of wine, five sheep already dressed, five seahs of roasted grain, one hundred clusters of raisins, and two hundred cakes of figs, and loaded them on donkeys. And she said to her servants, 'Go on before me; see, I am coming after you.' But she did not tell her husband Nabal." (1st Samuel 25: 18-19) Abigail made a quick decision to beg King David's forgiveness on behalf of her husband. Abigail went over her husband's head to obey her God. She recognized that it may not have been beneficial for her to speak to Nabal, and if she did not apologize for him, he was going to die.

Perhaps, if this woman who had been abused verbally reacted to this situation in an ungodly manner, she would have just watched David kill Nabal. Abigail placed her emotions to the side, and did not blame anyone else for her hurt. She saw beyond her drunken, abusive, and foolish husband and she still found the need to cover her husband and save his life. Would you have done what Abagail did if you in her situation? Would you have secretly smiled, and thanked God that this man who mistreats you daily will die? Perhaps, you would have just kept silent, and not tried to help him. Abigail placed her life on the line by approaching King David and his army of men in effort to spare the life of Nabal.

While David and his army of men were in route to slaughter Nabal, Abigail met them, presented all of gifts from her household and spoke to David, begging for her husband's life. King David was impressed because of Abigail's inner courage and outer appearance. It would be in one's best interest to take pattern after Abigail's example because there is so much power in our efforts to do the right thing. Unlike Abigail, a lot of times people veer from exercising the power in prayer.

There is power to change our lives, conditions and the lives of those who are around us when we enter the presence of God. We cannot become consumed by the bitterness of life's trials so much so that we fail to be the light in dark times. When we are going through trails, let us be spiritual about how we respond to the trial. If we gave a negative direct response to the circumstance, we would fail walking as Christians. Yes, bad situations can become painful, and I know that your relationship may have failed. Perhaps, you feel that your spouse may not deserve your prayers, love, wisdom or even your support. Indeed, if you are in a bad relationship, you may do the opposite of what Abigail did. You can blame anyone and everyone that you can think of for your unhappiness. I want you to know that as strange as this may sound, you are in control of your own happiness. You are in control of your own joy. Do not allow anyone to rob you of your joy. The scripture teaches us that we should not allow anyone to steal that which God has given us. Do not only be kind to those who are kind to you, but also pray for those who are evil towards you.

There is a difference between happiness and joy. Happiness is a feeling that comes and goes based on an action or an event. Joy is a gift of Eternity that God has placed within our hearts, and it allows us to feel good about ourselves and our lives during the good times as well as bad times. The Bible teaches us to have joy. Paul stated: "Not that I speak in respect of want: for I have learned, in whatsoever state I am, therewith to be content." (Philippians 4:11) The scripture is telling us to be content in all situations. Being satisfied with God, and the life that we have been granted is sometimes a challenge because there is always something more. The world is always advancing. There is always a bigger house, another choice for a spouse, a better car, a higher degree, and so forth. As people, we do not advocate contentment because the idea of something better appeals to us the most.

Abigail approached her husband the next day about what she had done. The scripture teaches us that she should have approached him that night, but he was drunk and she did not think it was a good idea. She wanted to speak with him once the wine had left his body, so she waited until the next day. Abigail told him that she had provided the lambs alongside additional gifts to six hundred men in King David's army. Surprisingly, when she spoke to her husband, Nabal did not degrade her, and he was not extremely nasty or bitter towards her. In fact, Nabal said nothing at all to Abigail for God had struck Nabal dead. Abigail was released of an abusive marriage. When King David heard of the news, he then sent his servants to propose marriage to Abigail, and she humbly accepted.

In conclusion, God gives us countless promises throughout his word. There are numerous times that he speaks through his living word, the Bible into our hearts and souls. I challenge you today to be the woman whom I know you can be. Be mindful of others, considerate, kind, and as beautiful on the inside as you are on the outside. Let us learn from the life of Abigail that we may practice not giving wrong for wrong. I pray that we do not respond to the bitter tragedies of life with more bitterness. Instead let us reach deep within our heart for holiness and sanctification. I pray that you apply love to your life, and give so much more to others than they give to you. I pray you be the woman that God has called you to be.

A Rose

You are a rose

Destined to bloom.

You are a rose

Full of life

If given room.

Beauty Is Skin Deep: A Discussion of Queen Esther

Vashti says no: "To bring before him Queen Vashti, wearing her royal crown, to display her beauty to the people and nobles, for she was lovely to look at. But when the attendants delivered the king's command, Queen Vashti refused to come. Then the king became furious and burned with anger" (Esther 1:11-12). Here, we find in the scripture Queen Vashti telling King Xerxes no, she will not be coming to see him and the nobles during their ongoing feast. Although it is not clearly stated why Vashti refused to appear, it could have been because the Queen would have been humiliated. In this text, Queen Vashti was told to appear, "wearing her royal crown," and one rabbinical tradition interprets this as the king's instruction to wear only her royal crown—in other words, she was told to appear nude. Based on tradition, Queen Vashti may have refused because she did not want to be put on display before a group of drunken kings.

Normally, whenever the King requests the presence of his Queen, she would humbly go because if she does not want to risk the consequence, which could be death. However, here we find when Vashti says no to the drunken King. The idea alone that Vashti told the King no is an astonishing one; it is an idea separate from the reality of how any other Queen would or could have responded to the King. My question to you is, "What happens when a Queen says no?" In this specific situation, King Xerxes had been drunk for many days. There was a continuous party or celebration that lasted for days, as written here, "And when these days were expired, the king made a feast unto all the people that were present in Shushan the palace, both unto great and small, seven days, in the court of the garden of the king's palace" (Esther 1:5) During the time when the king called for Vashti, and the other noble men of the court were drunk. Queen Vashti's appearance would have caused her to feel threatened, insecure, and violated.

We can apply this lesson to our lives because when we as woman feel threatened, violated, or uneasy for any reason, we must tell the world no. Do not be afraid to say no. Facing death as the possible penalty, Vashti told the King no. What are the things or people that you must say no to in your lives to keep your peace of mind? What are the situations, or habits that we must stand up against to win? Are we afraid of the consequences that follow our no, or are we bold enough to say no? The text is interesting because Vashti's refusal to see the King, stirred up an uproar in the courts. Vashti was removed, and the King's court immediately sought to replace the Queen; thus calling all of the virgins in Persia to come forward to the Kings court. This movement forever changed the Persian Empire. Because of Queen Vashti's refusal to see the King and his men, she was removed from the courts. The queen was replaced in an unprecedented action.

The story continues in the Book of Esther during the exile as Babylonians captivated the Jews. Sixty years after the capture of the Jews by Babylonians, the Persian Empire took over Babylonia. The Jews brought to Babylonia were captivated by the Persians. Here we have a foreigner in Persia, an orphan raised by her Uncle Mordecai. The young lady's name is Hadassah. The scripture teaches us about her physical attraction and her knowledge for the scriptures. It also teaches us how Mordecai feared that Hadassah would have been killed for being a Jew, so he gave her a name other than her Jewish: Esther. In this context, we will further discuss Hadassah, and refer to her as Esther.

Our creator made no mistakes on our color;

We are all beautiful despite our race, ethnicity or background.

Racism and prejudices are discussed in the Bible, particularly in the Book of Esther. Esther is used by God to rescue the Jews from the hands of the adversaries, who were the Persians. Esther was a Jewish orphan, who was given the name Esther by her uncle Mordecai to disguise her being a Jew. In the Book of Esther, a Jewish orphan becomes the Queen of a Persian Empire. Esther the Jew could have chosen to fear for her survival or life, but she was not afraid. Esther was bold, saying, "Go, gather together all the Jews that are present in Shushan, and fast ye for me, and neither eat nor drink three days, night or day: I also and my maidens will fast likewise; and so will I go in unto the king, which is not according to the law: and if I perish, I perish." We see Esther knew the Jewish people of Persia faced death because of their race. She willed to place herself at the hands of the King in effort to plea for the lives of her people. What tenacity Esther possessed to make such a firm decision to plea for her life and the sparing of all Jews in Persia.

As I reflect on the life of Esther, I want to ask, "What becomes of our future when we make small actions to fight for bigger things? What happens in our lives when we do not accept the bad news, but instead we plea and fight for good outcomes?" Although Esther was already Queen of Persia, the King still could have denied her request, but surprisingly, he did not. The king found beauty in Esther, which was skin deep, and he honored Esther's petition.

Like Esther, it is important that we find our superficial beauty. Find the glorious characteristics about yourself that lie in your personality and character. The Book of Esther does not only reference internal beauty, but also Proverbs 31:30 states, "Favour is deceitful, and beauty is vain: but a woman that feareth the Lord, she shall be praised." Throughout the Bible we discover various women. Some are alike and some are very different, but the Bible never changes its message about being complete and lovely, internally. Even in today's fast pace society, we must slow down and examine our hearts; we should ask ourselves, "How do I look inside my heart and in my mind." After all, humans see the outer appeal, but God sees the heart. I hope when God looks down on you and I, he sees loveliness, patience, kindness, meekness and so many more traits that are skin deep.

Whenever God provides us with a platform, status, or an opportunity to make a change, let us be like Queen Esther. Let us use the position to positively impact and enrich the lives of others. There are so many opportunities to give blessings forward. For example, Esther did not soak up her blessings and become oblivious of her past like so many of us would have done. She remembered, and she made a difference. Sometimes when we are promoted to certain levels regardless of if it is academia, career, or in life generally, we tend to want to be isolated and forgetful of those who are still in crisis. I know that making such choices may be the most comfortable, but these choices are not the most beneficial. Believers, we must be up and doing always. No level of success should be able to separate us from our purpose in God. Work, work, and more work! Allow God to use you while you are in the highest and even lowest position.

Regardless of our race, ethnicity, or background, each person will have a challenge to overcome to do something great. It is important that even in our challenges and experiences to yet serve God and those who are around us in a spirit of excellence. Greatness does require effort; it does not just coincidently happen. How many times in our lives are we challenged by obstacles because of our background or race? Esther could have allowed her being a Jew among Persians to stop her, but she did not allow this to be a barrier.

Such circumstances are not only demonstrated in the Book of Esther, but also in Acts. In Acts 6, although something great is happening such as the church is growing and multiplying, there came complaints. The complaint came from the Hellenist (Grecians), and was made towards the Jews. The Hellenist felt their widows were being overlooked during daily ministration which was the distribution of food. This is only one example of how cultural differences can create barriers within our place of worship if we allowed them to. Regardless of race, culture, or background, the Christian race is for everyone. Women, let us be great and love despite of differences.

They're Talking

Let them talk.

They don't know what they're talking about!

Hush!

I wish they would all hush,

And keep my name out of my mouth

Because what they are talking about wasn't my fault.

But their words hurt my pride

Causing tears to fill my eyes.

How I wish this pain was not a part of my life!

Hush!

Hush!

I wish they would hush!

I Was Raped and I Am Broken

Sometimes we experience bad times. We go through hardships, and people have so much to say about our circumstances while they are not even a part of our daily lives. It can be difficult to accept their words of wisdom, and even their comfort, when we know they do not understand our situation or we feel they cannot relate to us. Whenever we experience pain regardless of the depth of our pain, it brings a sense of blame on ourselves. This creates feelings of guilt and humiliation. This combination of emotions seems unbearable at times. Who do we run to? Who do we talk to when feel internally broken? Many times we have no one who to talk to even though we may be surrounded by family and friends. No matter what support we have, we may feel as though nobody will understand. I want to discuss a woman named Tamar who experienced these emotions because of a family member, and is ultimately turned away.

Tamar found herself victimized, robbed of her fidelity and confidence. Her purpose as she entered Amnon's bedroom was to serve. She was obedient and loyal to the request made by Amnon. Tamar believed Amnon was truly ill and needed to be served food; she was willing to oblige, as service is important. Often times as women, we may find ourselves in a vulnerable position such as this. How often do we only want to do what we are asked to do, or go where it is requested for us to go? In our obedience we may find that our vulnerability has been taken advantage of and there are few things as emotional or violating.

Like Tamar, providing a service makes so many women even in today's world feel valued. The Bible states that service is something we should provide. Everybody should be happy to partake in it, helping one another in an effort to better themselves. Whenever we dedicate ourselves and give our time and skills to a specific task, it makes us feel appreciated. Being in a position where we are able to help make situations better immediately causes us to reciprocate feelings of worthiness. This is because women are nourishers; we are designed to care, support, love, and aid in an ongoing fashion. For example, a woman bares and births a child. It is normal that she immediately makes a connection to care for her child. She will henceforth do almost anything to make sure her child survives and continues to succeed in life. In many cases, children reciprocate these feelings toward their mothers.

Such was the case with Tamar, though in a different relationship capacity. Tamar expected the reciprocity of her service provided to Amnon to be a feeling of reward. Instead, Tamar was left with grief, anguish, and pain because a man who rightfully should have protected her instead harmed and violated her.

Because service is worth providing, as women we should serve God, family, and our community the best we can. As we do so, however, we must exercise wisdom when doing so. We cannot answer every call or command that is given to us by others. Pray for wisdom. Constantly, ask God for his direction. Even in moments when a friend, loved one, or family member requests you to complete a task it is good to be careful and take one's own safety of ourselves. Service is needed, however, wisdom is required to guide you into making the best choices in life.

The definition of hurt is, "to cause pain or injury." It is most devastating when without warning the people whom we love and trust hurt us. The people whom we love, we begin to expect love from in return. These people can hurt us so easily. Subsequently, rapes unfortunately often occur at the hands of a family member. Hurt sometimes is an emotion that runs so deeply we do not understand it unless we have experienced it. Sometimes it runs so deeply we do not understand it even if we have experienced it.

Sometimes we are hurt so deeply during their childhood that the pain lies dormant within them, being carried into adulthood. Because of this, it is important to continuously pray that God not only protects us, but also delivers us from any hurt, pain or anger that may have been created within our hearts due to past and present situations.

Unfortunately, sin is something that can come from one generation to the next. While sin can create generational curses, this does not have to happen because we know and understand that God can deliver us of any evil that we may be experiencing. However, so often we notice in life that being young adults, we may struggle with the same issues that one or both of their parents struggled with. For example, if your mother is an alcoholic, you may struggle with alcoholism. If your father is abusive to his spouse, you may be abusive to your spouse. If you have a parent who is unfaithful to their spouse, you may be unfaithful to your spouse one day. This is of course not always true because sometimes we are framed by our parent's absence or made stronger and more significant people because of their failures.

Because sin can be passed down from one generation to the next, the Bible states in Lamentations 5:7, "Our fathers have sinned, and are not; and we have borne their iniquities." This scripture explains how the current generation is suffering because of the past generation. In further detail, the fathers and mothers actions caused the children to suffer. Suffering means to be cursed, or experience pain. There are mentions in the Old Testament of the Bible that discusses sin which may affect more than one generation. The Bible makes it clear that any curse can be broken and anyone who believes in Jesus Christ will only be accountable for their own sins, stating, "the fathers shall not be put to death for the children, neither shall the children be put to death for the fathers: every man shall be put to death for his own sin." (Deuteronomy 4:16) Throughout not only the Old Testament, but also the New Testament, the scripture echoes the power of forgiveness and how there is light is Jesus Christ. 2nd Corinthians 5:17 states, "Therefore if any man [be] in Christ, [he is] a new creature: old things are passed away; behold, all things are become new." When we are in Christ Jesus all of sins are forgiven and our weights are lifted. We no longer carry the sins and burdens of those in our family who lived before us because we are made free.

Certainly, this is great! It is amazing to know how we are made new. Unfortunately, although we made new in grace, many of times we choose to still live in bondages. Our mind is not free spiritually and mentally, and fails to allow ourselves to grasp freedom. Why is this? Amnon who fornicated and raped his sister Tamar, was the son David whom also was an adulterer and a murderer. Both David and Amnon struggled with sex and lust for women. The Bible states in 2nd Samuel 13:2 that Amnon developed a sickly love for Tamar: "And Amnon was so vexed, that he fell sick for his sister Tamar; for she was a virgin; and Amnon thought it hard for him to do anything to her." This is a type of sick love or lust in Amnon's heart. We know this because once Tamar entered Amnon's room and he had sex with her, the text states he hated her more than he ever loved her: "Then Amnon hated her exceedingly; so that the hatred wherewith he hated her was greater than the love wherewith he had loved her. And Amnon said unto her, Arise, be gone." (2nd Samuel 13:15) Here this man named Amnon, lusted until he was sick to have sex with Tamar, had sex with her, and afterwards he hated her more than he ever loved her. When I first read this text, I was amazed because so often men behave the same way even in today's society.

Father and son, David and Amnon lusted and acted on their lust. David, who is known as a King and hero in the Bible had several wives. Ahinoam of Jezreel, Abigail the Carmel, Maachah the daughter of King Talmai of Geshur, Haggith, Abital, and Eglah to name some; however, he still lusted for Bathsheba. He lusted for her so badly, that he ordered her husband to be placed on the front line of war, so he was killed, and he of course had sex with her, and later married her. Interestingly, David sinned against Bathsheba, but finds himself troubled when the Lord punishes his household, "Thus saith the Lord, Behold, I will raise up evil against thee out of thine own house, and I will take thy wives before thine eyes, and give them unto thy neighbor, and he shall lie with thy wives in the sight of this sun." (2nd Samuel 12:11)

If you are suffering because those who are near and related to you have chosen to live in the darkness, please understand that you can be removed from the circumstance. Maybe someone in your family has violated you. Perhaps it has just been rough dealing with all of the drama in your life. You do not have to live your life victimized, hurt, broken, and defeated. It is time for you to let the past go, and by faith grasp your future. Your future looks bright! You can do all things through Christ Jesus who strengthens you. You can even overcome your situation. Faith, courage, and wisdom are all inside of you! Move forward and upward!

Treasures In You

Secretly the storm is raging

And life is frightening.

Things appear to can't get worse

And words can't describe my hurt.

But somehow I close my eyes

I see your smile and hear your laugh.

Pain suddenly becomes a thing of the past...

My treasury's in you.

You bring me hope too.

My child; My hope; an extension of me.

Who'd ever knew I'd find such treasures in you?

From the very first moment I looked upon your face,

I knew my life was blessed with a new grace

And that the next step was predicated upon my faith.

I worked through trials to behold something great.

Treasures In You-continued

My endurance is worth the while.

Because of your precious smile

My treasury's in you.

You bring me hope too.

My child; my hope; an extension of me.

Who'd ever knew I'd find such treasures in you?

Protecting What Is Yours Story of Miriam and Moses

Protecting what is yours: Story of Miriam & Moses

The story of Miriam and Moses in the Bible is full of inspiration and other teachings that indicate the call of love in protecting what belongs to us. The sibling relationship between Moses and Miriam plays a vital role in understanding the happenings that faces the two as their story progresses in the bible. Miriam was Moses' older sister and daughter of Amar and Jockeyed. The role of Miriam in the life of Moses is one of the historical acts of courage and love that inspires many people to date. The growth of Moses is directly attached to deeds of two women; her sister Miriam and her mother.

When Moses was born, his mother placed him at the banks of Nile River in a basket to save his life. Pharaoh had decreed killing of all Hebrew baby boys. Moses' mother, therefore, hid her son, Moses, at the banks of a river and instructed Miriam to watch over Moses. Coincidentally, Pharaoh's daughter discovered the child (Moses) hidden by the river banks in a basket. It is the intervention of Miriam after the discovery that shows the love and protection she had towards his brother from Pharaoh's decree. It takes wisdom to protect families that God has given to women. According to the bible in the book of Exodus chapter two, Miriam quickly intervened when she realized that Pharaoh's daughter had discovered her brother. She wisely requested the princess to allow her to get a Hebrew woman to take care of the baby boy.

It turns out that Miriam gets her mother who is commanded by Pharaoh's princess to take care of Moses and bring him back when he grows older. This is a classic example of family commitment. It demonstrates miles that women can go to protect what God has given them. Although Miriam was a young girl when she was facing pharaoh's daughter, her age did not limit her from saving her brother Moses. The actions of Moses' mother also illustrate the unceasing effort that women should put in protecting the family. She did the best to save the life of her son.

In the contemporary world, it takes interminable effort to protect families, finances or dreams that God has given to women. Several research findings indicate that progress in human civilization is eroding family principles. The cases of family disintegration regarding infidelity, separation or even divorce are on the increase. What are women roles in protecting families and marriages? In the book of Genesis, God is the founder of marriage. We read, "And the Lord God said, it is not good that the man should be alone; I will make him a help meet for him" (Genesis 2:18, King James Version). It is God who started families and marriages and women have a role in protecting these social institutions. It may not be easy to defend God's gifts to women. Just like Miriam did to save his brother Moses, it takes sheer determination and audacity to protect what God has given to us.

As we progress in the evaluation of the story of Miriam and Moses, it demonstrates the role of women leadership in protecting their gifts from God. God used Moses and Miriam to direct the Israelites from the land of slavery to Canaan. Although Moses and Miriam did not make it to the Promised Land, Miriam's role in the journey to Canaan is evident after Israelites crossed red sea. The bible describes Miriam as a prophetess who broke into song and dance after God had saved Israelites at the red sea. She sang, "And Miriam answered them, Sing ye to the LORD, for he hath triumphed gloriously; the horse and his rider hath he thrown into the sea" (Exodus 15:21, King James Version).

The story of Miriam and Moses also illustrates an essential lesson on grumbling against those we love. Miriam had a role to be an example in demonstrating family love. Unfortunately, at some point, she started complaining against her brother Moses who had married a Cushite woman. The Bible records Miriam inquiring whether God can only speak to Moses. She wonders why God cannot also speak through them (Miriam and Aaron). It is catastrophic to grumble against our families or other precious gifts that God has given to us. The consequences of this evil act can haunt our lives just like Miriam came to learn later. When God became angry with Miriam for complaining against his brother who was God's servant, he struck her with Leprosy.

It is evil and dangerous to complain or hate when God appoints, blesses or prospers other people or our relatives. As women, we should love what God has blessed or given to us. Jealousy is a vice that can find its way in hearts of many women as demonstrated by the story of Miriam and Moses. Women should be watchful always to guard against the temptations that come to steal the joy of what God has given them in their lives. It is also important to be prayerful at all the times since many challenges can face our families, goals or other God's gifts in our lives. Prayers can save lives of those we love. When leprosy struck Miriam, her brother Moses prayed for her healing which saved her life. "And Moses cried unto the LORD, saying, Heal her now, O God, I beseech thee." (Numbers 12:13, King James Version). It is God's will to protect what is ours.

Strengthen The Good That Remain

Pain harness,

But I refer to Revelations 3:2

To strengthen that which remain.

Things won't stay the same.

No, change must come

But until then

I plan to wait.

Although pain harness,

I plan to stay bless.

I can't feel the change,

But I know to strengthen the good that remain.

When God Speaks To A Woman A Discussion of Deborah

The name of Deborah is of great importance in scripture. It is written in Judges 4:4-5 that Deborah was "the prophetess, the wife of Lapidoth, was judging Israel at that time. And she would sit under the palm tree between Ramah and Bethel in the mountains of Ephraim. And the children of Israel came up to her for judgment" (Judges 4:4.5, The New King James Version). It is not strange in the contemporary American Society to be a female leader. Though, it does not contradict the desires of God. He has the plan concerning women and it is evident in the story of Deborah. As it was written before, Deborah was the prophetess, and she was not the only women among men who were that close to God.

God used the talents of Deborah to help the others in the most difficult situations. The passage when He calls her to speak to Barak is one of such examples. It was written in the Scripture that Deborah told Barak that "Has not the LORD God of Israel commanded, saying, 'Go and deploy troops at Mount Tabor; take with you ten thousand men of the sons of Naphtali and of the sons of Zebulun" (Judges 4:6, The New King James Version).

She was not leading the army, but she gave the man who actually was the military leader the motivation to move. She reminded him of his duties. As Christian Women in the modern world, it is important to stand beside your husband and give him strength in critical situations. It is the anointing that God gives women to be able to fast and pray, and even give instruction. It is the altruistic commitment, which is very valuable; however, sometimes the mission of the woman is underestimated. If you often feel that you are likely to give up, because this path is too difficult, and no one understands how hard you try, remember that God sees you and supports.

Thus, the story of Deborah shows that God loves women and wants them to serve Him in a special way. Women need to believe in themselves and to find the inner strength which allows them to help God in their own manner. The point whether she has the attention of others, or prefer to do it secretly is not as important as obedience to God's word. Every woman needs to remember to allow God to instruct and guide them in their doings just as Deborah enacted in the scripture. God gives us grace when we obey him even if that means allowing him to speak through us.

I Dwell In You

I dwell in you.

I'm in your heart.

Forsake not the assembly,

But when you pray remember me.

It's all about what's inside the human soul

That creates the church universal.

God is not a building.

Instead, he dwells inside the hearts of humans.

Be Hospitable: A Shunammite Woman Blesses Elisha

Looking at the story of the Shunammite woman and the prophet named Elisha helps us to see how the story relates to the lives of women in the aspect of being hospitable. The case Shunammite woman acts as a practical example of people who have a welcoming heart. Through this story it becomes evident that our actions lead us to a righteous life.

In Second Kings 4:8-10, there was a day when Elisha went to Shunem. There he found a woman whom insisted to bless him. She desired that he would stay for a meal and whenever Elisha passed through the village that he stopped at her and her husband's house. The woman did not make these actions in the absence of her husband; she had already informed him that the man that usually comes to their home is Holy, and he is Man of God. She went on and suggested that they reserve a small room for him where he can stay when he comes. Although the scripture does not provide the woman's name, her message is revealed clearly. Concerning what she can do well is revealed, yet she's married. The glimpse of her character is seen right from the beginning.

It is amazing that she knew that Elisha was faithful to God and she was willing to help him. The request she made to her husband was considered, and a room was given to him. The prophet requested to talk to the king so that the woman could be brought to him. Then Gehazi told Elisha that she had no child. It is prophesied to the woman that about this time in the coming year you will have a child in your hands. The woman was so surprised when she heard this, but she believed the Prophet. As time went, she got pregnant and delivered a baby boy just as the prophet had told her.

As all of this occurred, life went on as usual. There were tears of joy when the baby was conceived, and from the Bible, the scripture goes on and tell us that the boy grew. But all of a sudden, there are untold circumstances that happened as it is shown in Second Kings 4:19 that an accident was incurred and the boy died on the laps of his mother. From this incident, it is better to put ourselves in the place of this woman. The child died at a younger age; however, the woman never doubts God. As the story goes on, we can see that this woman did not lose hope and she was indeed strong, which is the same message that women should consider. In Second King 4:23, the woman even stated that all was well: "And he said, "Why will you go to him today? It is neither new moon nor Sabbath." She said, "All is well;" thus, the woman's characteristics exemplified courage and faith. Knowing that her son had died, she stated all is well. How many of us can do that? The reason she was able to state that all is well is because she her faith in God and in the prophet of God had already affirmed that the circumstance would have been resolved as God sees best.

Everyone can imagine how the woman's heart felt at that moment. After learning that her son was deceased, the woman laid the body in the room that was given to Elisha, and then she went to look for him at Mount Carmel. She took the donkey and the servant and said to the servant that lead on; "please do not be slow unless I tell you." This message indicates that she was a woman of mission, which is a good lesson to all women. Despite our circumstances, we should be focused on the outcome. After she reached where Elisha was located at that time, she asked him to help her to heal the sick child. The distance that this woman traveled implied that she was not reluctant to give up on her son. Imperatively, she desired to see her child well even without thinking of the challenges she could go through to attain it. One can learn from this incident that; whenever problems get us, and we lead a righteous life like that of this woman, the Lord's will is always the solution to our problems.

The prophet ordered the servant to put his staff on the face of the boy since the mother could not leave Elisha. They tried all this, but the boy could not come back, then later he went to the room where they had kept the boy and closed the door and prayed not until the boy came back to life. When the woman heard of this, she bowed at the feet of Elisha and then took the son. Here the woman shows that she had hope in God. Therefore, this is a lesson to all women that no matter how the problem could be, always have pray and seek Godly counsel. Through this woman we see actions of hospitality, and perseverance. These are the same traits that can help us through our walk of life.

Sister, Live and Live Again

You are so beautiful; you are in control

Of the things you do and say and the places you go.

When your best is not enough, remember God knows Math.

He knows how to take your grief and make you laugh.

If your hips grow wide or level thin,

You are still beautiful because of God's love within.

If you cannot find reason to live

Because of the pain that grows within,

Remember I say to you:

Live and live again.

By the way don't think that I haven't made light of a darkened day.

We are all so much alike

Sister, Live and Live Again- continued

And sorrow is a theme of life...

Regardless if she beside you mention the truth

Or escape it like others do-

We're all just humans inside tugging from the darkness trying to find the light.

We all are wanting something more,

Or searching for the next detour.

But we must choose to end the pain.

We must choose love and live,

And if you cannot find a reason to live

Because of the pain that grows within

Remember I said to you:

Live and live again!

Conclusion

We are women, and we were created by God's craftsmanship. We come from all walks of life, and throughout history we can find women in and out of the Bible whom we can relate to ourselves. The key to being a conqueror and a winner is to keep going, never give up. and be constant in prayer. I challenge you to purify your life, and take time to communicate with God. Once you have spent weeks or months using the chart mentioned in Chapter 1, and have asked God to purify your life, heart and soul, pray and ask God to reveal to you what is your purpose for life. Prayer, fasting and simply making time in our busy schedules is so important as a growing believer. I challenge you to look at the women discussed in this book, and reflect upon who you are and whom you pray to become.

Again, life can be challenging. Trust me, I know life is filled of ups and downs. However, as a woman, I want you to develop and own solitude. Do not allow people to dictate who you are in life. Learn your identity through connecting with God, and live out your purpose through life. Take on challenges, and win new victories each day. Learn who you are, discover yourself through fasting and praying while having patience with God to reveal himself to you. Remember, despite your circumstances, you are a winner.

In conclusion, I love to see myself in other women. It makes me smile. Regardless if it is a mother, a grandmother, an aunt, great-aunt, cousin, or mentor. The reason is because I am encouraged and inspired by what I can accomplish whenever I see myself in other women. Whenever I hear of their testimonies, and learn of the trials that they have overcome, still rising to success, it inspires me. There may be a situation that I have gone through that can potentially help or encourage you. There may be something you have done that inspires me. We must be nurturing to one another as women. Always remember, Being A Woman Is An Art!

www.ingramcontent.com/pod-product-compliance
Lightning Source LLC
Chambersburg PA
CBHW032134090426
42743CB00007B/596